# The Forbidden Lunchbox
## and Other Poems

### Richard Modiano

Punk 愛 Hostage 愛 Press

**The Forbidden Lunchbox and Other Poems**
Copyright © Richard Modiano 2022
An imprint of Punk Hostage Press
ISBN: 978-1-940213-23-1

All rights reserved. Printed in the United States of America. No part of this text may be used or reproduced in any manner whatsoever without written permission from the author or publisher except in the case of brief quotations embodied in critical articles and reviews. For information address Punk Hostage Press.

**Edited by
S.A. Griffin**

**Cover Layout
S.A. Griffin**

**Punk Hostage Press**
Hollywood, USA
punkhostagepress.com

For

Danny Baker (1969 – 2020)
Janet Miller (1950 – 2020)
Vincent Zangrillo (1955 – 2020)

## Titles and First Lines

Note to Self.................................................................................................2
At the Rainbow Bar & Grill .......................................................................3
Comrade ....................................................................................................5
L.A. River Flows .......................................................................................6
On the Way to Work NYC ........................................................................7
Drops fall ...................................................................................................9
At the Subway Station .............................................................................10
L.A. is Burning........................................................................................11
A Hole in the Air.....................................................................................12
Subway Train Manhattan Evening ..........................................................13
Transcontinental Bus Trip While Reading Evolution Book ....................14
A Thousand and One ...............................................................................16
Excerpt from Vita Sexualis .....................................................................17
Senryu I-II ...............................................................................................18
Haiku I-IV ...............................................................................................18
Drive All the Horses at Once ..................................................................19
Bela Lugosi's Accomplishments .............................................................21
Lion of Dharma .......................................................................................22
On the Streets of the Lower East Side.....................................................23
Poem for Danny Baker ............................................................................24
Poem for Dennis Cruz .............................................................................25
Poem for Zoë Tamerlis............................................................................26
Swayambu Stupa .....................................................................................27
Kamo River Mid-autumn ........................................................................30
Things are not what they appear to be, nor are they otherwise ...............31
Gaijin.......................................................................................................32
Peace Plaza, Hiroshima ...........................................................................34
A Man Who Lost His Hair and Died Bleeding .......................................36
The Forbidden Lunch Box ......................................................................37
Student Uniform ......................................................................................38
Tricycle....................................................................................................39
Mother, Mother .......................................................................................40
Geta (Wooden Sandal) ............................................................................41
謎々 (Nazonazo) A Bar in Hiroshima .....................................................42
On the Lid of an Urn ...............................................................................43
Los Judíos Sefardíes Regresan ................................................................45

| | |
|---|---|
| To Persevere | 47 |
| Anthropocene | 49 |
| More! More! More! | 50 |
| MAGA MAGA | 51 |
| OBVIOUSLY, GENTLEMEN | 52 |
| Twisted in Blood and Nerve | 53 |
| Trumpenvolk | 55 |
| The Perfect Ones | 56 |
| How Do You Want to Die? | 57 |
| It comes to you in small… | 59 |
| Endgame | 60 |
| You who no longer dance in the street | 61 |
| Capitulation is necessary only when struggle has become completely | 62 |
| Rimbaud knew better than | 64 |
| Wage Slave | 65 |
| FOR/AGAINST | 66 |
| Go Underground | 69 |
| You can taste it in the shock and roar | 70 |
| After the Cataclysm | 73 |
| Scott Wannberg: Poet and Cinephile | 75 |
| El Matador | 77 |
| Poem for Rob Plath | 78 |
| A Word | 79 |

# Foreword

These are all of the poems that I could find or gather that I think are worth preserving in a book. There are three lineages of prosody that are most resonant with me, the Haikai lineage of Japanese poetry, the Surrealist lineage, and the Beat lineage with its antecedents in Objectivist, Imagist and Projective verse, and I have written poems that I hope are worthy contributions to my sources of inspiration. There are also some short prose pieces that point to people and ideas that brought me to poetry and sustained my commitment. The newest poems were written during the COVID-19 pandemic and the final days of the Trump Administration, and after a series of overlapping personal blows and disappointments. Others are drawn from the past 35 years of my life on the planet with all the epiphanies and travails therewith.

– **Richard Modiano**

## Author's Acknowledgements

Some of these poems were published in *1870, Amass Magazine, The Artifa[ctuals], Big Scream, Blue Satellite, The Cultural Weekly, Dashboard Horus, Dear Bela, Escape Wheel, GAS: Poetry, Art & Music, Heroin Love Songs 2.0, Maintanent, Malpais Review, Mas Tequila Review, Out of the Fire, Oxygen: Parables of the Pandemic, The Patterson Review of Literature, Sun Flowers and Locomotives,* and *Three Times 3.*

Thanks to Will Alexander, Danny Baker (late), Ronee Blakely, Bob Branaman, Peter Carlaftes, Michael Casares, Kalpna-Singh Chitnis, David Cope, Dennis Cruz, Yago Cura, Alexis Rhone Fancher, Amelie Frank, Rich Ferguson, Thomas Fucaloro, Nelson Gary, Kat Georges, Maria Mazziotti Guillen, Aris Janigian, Susan Hayden, Jack Henry, Marie C Lecrivain, ML Liebler, Rick Lupert, Viggo Mortensen, Harry Northup, John O'Kane, Marc Olmsted, Jane Omerod, Puma Perl, Rob Plath, A. Razor, Margaret Randall, Belinda Subraman, Susan Suntree, Pat Thomas, Richard Vargas, George Wallace, Scott Wannberg (late), Pam Ward, Marc Zegans and Mike Zone.

Special thanks to Iris Berry for 27 years of poetry comradeship and friendship.

My good friend S.A. Griffin was a dream editor, and his patience, encouragement and attunement has substantially benefited these pieces. I am grateful beyond words.

# Introduction

Relevant, vivid, deliciously explicit, Modiano, king of LA's literary scene, time-travels internationally from coffee shops to bars occupying the space between lipstick women sitting alone to intimate portraits of Bukowski and Bela Lugosi. Scenarios seemingly mundane spring from the page, rich, well-paced poems flow somewhere near LA's River, where hospital rain drips, where "sleep is buried in caves inhabited by lemurs," or live in the atomic lunchboxes of Hiroshima. Written in a sparse, frantic clip, both complicated and engaging, this master of the gemstone phrase, "feral cats calling for mates," Modiano's approaches the poem like a thief you don't see coming, calmly, quietly arresting, with verse that burns, electrifies the mind, "hiding inside the flame of a single match, waiting to set fire to your dead body."

Pam Ward, author *Want Some Get Some, Bad Girls Burn Slow*

"…if tears shall wash away the cruelty of our years, and sow the seeds of pity in our black and broken hearts, remind us that life is brief and lovely, not long and foolish, that it is strange and beautiful, yea as a dream, then so let it be, if it must be tears, if tears alone may serve…"

~ Jack Kerouac

## Note to Self

If you've never doubted the integrity of your
superiors or their right to demand your obedience
nor felt the sting of wishing for something that
could not be found on department store shelves
or voting ballots –

If you've never fallen so deeply in love that it
seemed that you had been sleep walking through life
until that moment –
never daydreamed desperately
in a board meeting or on the job
never been carried away by extremities of emotion while
everyone around you remained unmoved and oblivious –

If you've never suspected that real life
must be elsewhere
somewhere beyond the shopping malls and the suburbs
off the highway
over the fields and oceans –

If there is no part of you unfulfilled by
stock options and prime time programming and
cutting edge digital technology –
then perhaps these poems are not for you

## At the Rainbow Bar & Grill

Sitting in the upstairs
bar of the Rainbow next to
a good looking woman waiting
for my friends—

The bar tender isn't
bad looking either—I like
her lipstick—

The good looking
woman wears no make-up
but her fingernails
are long and red—

She drinks
a glass of red wine—

The bartender sets a glass and
a bottle of mineral water before me—

The good looking woman says,
"Whatcha writin'?"

She has smooth
ebony skin, straight
shoulder-length black hair
parted down the middle,
brown eyes under long
lashes—

"I'm drafting an
article for my private
newspaper"

"Yeah? Where's it published?"

"In my mind"

She touched my ring
finger with her index finger
and stroked it with
her red painted nail—

"No wedding ring?"

"No wedding ring"

She smiled—

My friends arrived, my
girlfriend arrived and
I gripped my glass with my
left hand—

I got up and greeted
my friends and put my arm
around my girlfriend—

The good looking woman slid off the barstool
walked over to
me and pulled my sleeve so
I leaned toward her and she
whispered in my ear,
"Relationships, such a
ball and chain"

"Yes, you have a
nice night too" I said

**Comrade**

I like to read and write in coffee shops
old habit, escape from noisy lodgings of bygone days---
I share the place with the gentrified locals
fixated on glowing screens if alone
yakking about what's cool if with others
talking about dreams of screenplays and auditions
with the eagerness of youthful promise---
they pay me no mind, the old fellow
in threadbare clothes scribbling in a pocket notebook with a fountain pen---
The young barista
pierced, braided, tattooed took
the money and handed me a coffee
as we made the exchange, I said cheerily, "Thanks, comrade."
Leaning in and glancing side to side conspiratorially,
the barista whispered back, "How did you know I was a communist?"

## **L.A. River Flows**

One brown duck and two ducklings swim downstream
brackish LA River water
late summer morning under overcast skies

LA River's water is always flowing
even when there's a drought
a thin trickle flows
where the concrete wall meets the concrete floor

Stones, trees, houses, city blocks flow too
human beings flow culture flows

The sound of water flowing is the sound of time and the water of time
glimmers on the river bed of the universe


8/28/01 Moorpark St. Bridge near Fulton St. Sherman Oaks

## On the Way to Work NYC

Good morning you will be loved

On this glorious day

You will be hated, both

Kissed and despised


Good

Morning sun bright steps rising

To brownstone buildings

Chic yuppie businesswoman, eager

Young black boy totting his athletic bag Sour middle-aged rent-a-cop angling

Down sun shiny steps to the subway train

Sadly heedlessly or inspired

Reckless on this glorious

Day you will love you will hate both

Kiss and despise

The exotic beauty the radiantly ugly

The genius or the just plain foolish and goofy Good morning all!

On this glorious day the boundless

Blue beret is on you lovely heads go ahead

Love and be loved hate and be hated kiss And despise be kissed and despised!

– 5/88 Lower Manhattan, NYC

**Drops fall**
>from the iron railing
>>outside the hospital
>>>where my brother lies
>>>>dying---
>>>>>Spring rain

*– 4/6/88 NYC*

## At the Subway Station

      A young man approaching
        and a woman, turning her back
     on him without a word, and
going out to the sidewalk
A man in a sudden outburst of anger
    at a woman who appears to
        have come late for their date
A group of girl students, each
    hand in hand with a friend, their free hands
separately
    hailing a taxi
A plump middle-aged woman
      approaching with rapid
    mincing steps
Every face looking totally intent on some
    immediate intimate aim ---

What I noticed
    coming from
        the death bed of my brother

    – 4/8/88

## L.A. is Burning

I walk to the edge of night
where sleep is buried in little caves inhabited by lemurs,
their eyes frozen like electrocuted goldfish.
I yank one of them out by the tail and instantly the cave crumbles,

the tail changes into a rope of fire that won't let go of my hand--
I realize this means opportunity:
Go and settle old scores, a voice tells me. Set fire to the stores, to the banks, to the unloved ones—


then burrow yourself deep into dreams.

## A Hole in the Air

You open your savage breasts two
birds who have been wronged fly
out of you one is black
and stares into your eyes where
the other is red you are waiting
for a joust
you are a goddess demanding a carnival of
carnage hungering to witness little beaks
tearing each other for the poisoned feather
you wave in your hand when the blood
begins to rise you announce there will be no
victor the two savage
birds are really angels who are already
dead moreover just figments of the
imagination
evil
is a hole in the air that has not been
invented for as you pronounce your
verdict without saying a word
the two birds fly back into you
as if by magic you are no longer there

## Subway Train Manhattan Evening

A young office worker hanging onto a strap Another sitting on a seat

Another swaying with the sway

Under gloomy electric lights

Who you are nobody knows Getting off at your station

There are times of riding beyond

The station & coming back again

Who you are even you don't know

Your exhausted silk necktie--- Inside of its knot

Something you do not realize is hiding

If you think it over well

You will come to realize what it is

It is hiding inside the flame of a single match Waiting to set fire to

your dead body

*– 10/87 NYC IRT subway*

## Transcontinental Bus Trip While Reading Evolution Book

West of Denver
      fossil rodents appear suddenly
           fog & snow, superhighway
Clods of dirt
      reading Hitching on Evolution
           the Central Electric Supply Co.
Watson & Crick, 1953
      crystalline spirals of DNA
           coded info only out to protein
                molecular "how" of heredity
Schnooky's Cookies
     wire fence
          romantic in water vapor

Baby cries in seat ahead
      Precambrium jump from bacteria
           camping phone next right
                genetic drift in fruit flies

Black on yellow diamond bicycle
      lovers fight
            about their children

Simultaneous unrelated advantageous mutations
Clear Creek Canyon
           Marcel Scbutzenberger scientist says
              "no leaps in nature"

Idaho Springs
      Self-serve---no smoking
           Sun races west, into blue sky
130 million light-sensitive rods and cones
      Next rest stop Silver Plume
           system of coordinated variables
Firewood for Sale
      Continental Divide
           Push here toexit

     *– 3/89 Highway 80 western states*

## A Thousand and One

I'd dreamed of a Greyhound pick up every time I made the NYC to SF run and it finally happened at the Cheyenne Wyoming two-hour layover, the station next to the red brick two story hotel. It was the on the day of 100$^{th}$ anniversary when Custer bite the dust at the Greasy Grass. She was on her way to a casino job at Stateline.

The room was small and when we sat on the edge of the bed it sank at least a half foot, the other side rising by an equal amount with the accompanying protest of old springs. It was a second-floor room with spare but neat furnishings and the stale odor of cigarettes. The yellowed blinds were up and I could see a metal grate over the one window. If there was a fire, we'd be trapped like lobsters in a cage if we didn't get out the door fast enough.

The bathrooms in old hotel rooms are always the most depressing. This one was slightly larger than the phone booths I saw at every gas station along the route. Sink, toilet and shower stall all complete with matching rust stains were set in a crowded configuration. If you were ever sitting on the toilet when somebody came in, you'd lose your kneecaps.

We looked at each other for a long moment, each waiting for the other to make the first move. Finally, I did, stepping close to her and pulling her into a long kiss. We broke off, and over her shoulder I looked at the worn yellow bed spread where a thousand people had lain and fucked. We undressed. She was a natural blonde.

"Are you Jewish?" she joked.
"Yes."
"I thought you were Italian." She was chagrined.
"A common mistake. The name sounds Italian."

**Excerpt from Vita Sexualis**

Introduction: One of the few useful services performed by the subaltern class of British colonial administrators in India was the retrieval and translation of certain Sanskrit texts which otherwise might have been lost to posterity. Some of these texts dealt with erotic matters, and the canon of propriety of the era would not permit the direct translation of these passages into English; instead, they were rendered in Latin.

We here present a translation into English of Simon Newton's (1859 – 1919) Latin translation of Dharmandamoksha's (1251 – 1333) *Vita Sexualis* (circa 1227):

Cunnilingus is characterized by the swarming of bees, a frozen tongue, an elastic statue leaning into a pool of fire, a Madonna's eyebrow exploding in a photograph at the edge of an iceberg where only ducks are allowed into the drawing room of intercourse, three bears chained to the rancid odor of a zookeeper's hand, 36 mice in the keys of a piano, 14 flashlights, 19 ravens, 16 heating pads, a gun, a knife, a vacation in the desert.

## Senryu I

Eating warm peaches on a hot day
        Eating pussy

## Senryu II

In the parking lot of Burger King
        The odor of the stock yard

## Haiku I

Iron skillet rusting
        In rank summer grass—
The peeling clapboard cottage

## Haiku II

Late afternoon ---
        Reading in the easy chair
              No cat in my lap

## Haiku III

        Dawn breaks over the East River
The poet takes a picture --
        Insomnia

## Haiku IV

In the bough of the sick avocado tree
        the feral cat cries for her mate—
            Autumn nightfall

**Drive All the Horses at Once**

One Saturday afternoon in the autumn of 1967 I was visiting the Dialog Bookshop on Fulton Avenue in Van Nuys California. The bookshop was across the street from the campus of Valley Junior College (now called San Fernando Valley Community College,) and students browsed the shelves afternoon and evening (it stayed open until 9:00 on Friday and Saturday.) I was a 16 year old high school student, and the Dialog was the store to visit for underground newspapers, obscure literary magazines as well as political and pacifist periodicals.

The store had a bulletin board where notices of local anti-war rallies, informal study groups, rock concerts, be-ins and love-ins and poetry readings were posted. I saw a flyer for a Sunday afternoon reading in Echo Park with a list of poets scheduled to read, among them Charles Bukowski. I followed his column "Notes of a Dirty Old Man" that was published in *Open City* a Los Angeles- based underground weekly (later it appeared in the *Los Angeles Free Press* after *Open City* folded.) I also read some of his broadsides in the store since I couldn't afford to buy them.

Two high school friends who also dug poetry knew about the reading, and one of them had a car so we drove to the Echo Park reading a week later. The reading was held a private residence and the host was the poet John Thomas. In fact, it was his house where the reading was held. I didn't know who John Thomas was and I'd never seen Bukowski, and in the small living room Thomas seemed to take up most of the space. Meantime, sitting on the floor with his back to the wall was a man who was sipping Brew 102 from a can, a partially finished 6 pack between his legs (Brew 102 was a local Los Angeles beer that sold for 75 cents a six pack.) To his right was a reel-to-reel Webcor tape recorder.

John Thomas read some fine work and was followed by another poet whose name I don't remember, and then by an exotic looking woman with red hair. Finally, Thomas said, "Our next reader is Charles Bukowski." The man sitting on the floor pressed the start button and we listened to 4 pre-recorded poems while Bukowski continued to sip his beer. Even then Bukowski didn't like reading in public. I don't remember what poems he read but I do remember liking them a lot and thinking that I too could write poetry if only I knew how.

After the reading I went up to Bukowski and kneeled next to him and asked, "Mr. Bukowski, what do you have to know to be a good poet?" He answered, "Kid, you have to know how to drive all the horses at once."

## Bela Lugosi's Accomplishments

He backed the communist revolution of Bela Kuhn Hungary 1919 but was never black listed in Hollywood
He spoke "beast language" in *Murders In the Rue Morgue* horror movie 30 years before Michael McClure
He starred in a Broadway show & spoke his lines phonetically to acclaim -- the critics couldn't tell
World War I wound pain-killer morphine addiction 40 years duration -- he cleaned up & died sober

1968 I worked as movie extra Universal Pictures lot of monster movie fame
One night dreamt I met him on the set
Mr. Lugosi," I said, "You Taught me how to behave with dignity"
He smiled


– Written in Bela Lugosi's last residence, 12/98

## Lion of Dharma

The leisurely ants are laboring to drag away the
          corpse of a dead bee --
The spring sparrows are perching side by side
          on a plum tree branch --
The *domesticas,* drawn and tired, sit on the bus
          holding purses in their laps --
The middle school boys are riding skate-boards
          down the middle of the sidewalk
                heedless of pedestrians --
Allen Ginsberg the Lion of Dharma is dead
          his soft roar echoes
                in my thoughts

*– 4/5/97*

## On the Streets of the Lower East Side
　　*– for Puma Perl*

Sing in me Muse, and through me tell the story--
On the streets of the Lower East Side
fearless knowledge appeared
like a natural angel
at the bottom of her heart
On the streets of the Lower East Side
fearless knowledge sought her
with searchlights shining
to the bottom of her heart
On the streets of the Lower East Side
fearless knowledge of the night and what it does to you
filled her soul
with the stunning brilliance
On the streets of the Lower Eastside
Fearless knowledge exhaled
in her words
with the force of a truth gale
that blew us away
Fearless knowledge
her life raft for that January grief
Fearless knowledge
bought from insomnia
turned into art
"The pictures take themselves"

Fearless knowledge
of our capacity to hurt
of our potential to love
of our creative generosity
fearless knowledge
Puma's knowledge
shared with us
our knowledge
fearless knowledge

## Poem for Danny Baker

The world of real life, the raw urgency of the moment--
the taste of black coffee, of charred red meat,
the recoil of the Glock in your hand, the poem that forms in your brain--
waits for us beneath history,
its mysteries passed down through
generations in the currency of moments
so intense they annihilate time itself,
moments that can be suppressed, discouraged and denied by
the rules, laws, and regulations that hem us in from every side.

We adventurers track these moments through this world
as hunters track the most prized of prey.
As long as we have hearts in our chest
we will find ways to them again and again.

History is haunted by its own karma--
the moment of freedom, of real poetry
brings all its unsettled debts back into play,
to be discharged forever so life can really begin.

What we want now are moments so overwhelming,
so irresistible that
the entire control system of regulated life
melts before their scorching radiance

**Poem for Dennis Cruz**
    – inspired by *The Beast is We*

I saw a black tarantula crawling out from under the flower pots
Have you ever seen one?
They are not spiders
They are black and furry and beautiful because
When ugliness and wickedness are as deep as existence
When they come down from eternity they have a perfection of their own—

I watched this beast and I said to myself,
How beautiful you can be with your long strangler's paws
Your fine corset of dusky velvet
Your furry belly, your fabulous jaws
It was when a big drop of poison fell, that's how you were born
And you live because you are perfect—

But I'm going to take my revenge on you filthy insect
I've known too many victims and I have a debt to pay
And just imagine, the tarantula understood me
He was paralyzed, befuddled by his destiny
He looked around stupidly for a way out, but for him
There was no way, my eyes hypnotized him—

I was so sure that he wouldn't go away
That I went into the kitchen for the hammer
It gave me pleasure to swing the hammer on the black beast
And I laughed as though I'd had one drink too many—
I crushed the velvet tarantula with one blow crack!
That's what you've got to do from time to time in this world
Or the air would be unbreathable

## Poem for Zoë Tamerlis

Cats leap across my heart when I
see your full red lips
and the glassy water breaks
with white sparks
scattering your words in all directions
Zoë your crowned scalp
with inky black hair
a halo of dawn over the urban river's
skyline
tonight you see through my words
Zoë of twilight ruby
and I sleep through your breath
Zoë of black leather
I dream through your tattooed arms
Zoë of a desert where the hawks
turn blue
and I walk in your palm of
Mt. Meru
Zoë of obsidian in the coup d'état
and I'm lost in your solar
breasts the flares made fertile
Zoë in the night of honeysuckle
Zoë of crystal palace
Zoë of Mongolian steppes covered
with gold Krugerrands
Zoë of boots under a redbrick
tenement where anarchists are
plotting our liberation
Zoë of dolphin spume
Zoë of lava made helium
Zoë

*– 4/21/20*

**Swayambu Stupa**
    *– for Nelson Gary*

I.

The gilded dome of Swayambu Stupa---
    it's painted eyes gaze over
        the Nepalese capital of Katmandu---
Behind the stupa is
    a nondescript building
        with a single shabby room
empty but for a bronze door
    smeared with vermilion powder---
        Some people believe this door
leads to a cave where
    a passage way descends to
        a subterranean lake
where the Indian sage Nagarjuna
    was taken by a species of sub-aquatic serpents
        called nagas to retrieve the Buddha's *Wisdom*
*Discourses*---
Through meditating on these forgotten and hidden teachings
    Nagarjuna discovered how to understand
        the terrifying and fascinating
Emptiness that quivers beneath the threshold of common sense ---
    Nagarjuna returned to terra firma
        to reveal what he had learned ---
Today the door of the cave is locked and bolted ---
    Once a year it is opened by a Newari Buddhist priest
        who enters to perform religious rites ---
Rumors abound of yogis suspended in meditation
    and curious pilgrims who have entered
        never to return

II.

In the ThamalBahal
    a rambling and dilapidated temple and school
        inthe center of Katmandu

some ancient scriptures are preserved
> stored under lock and key
>> and wrapped in endless layers of cotton cloth and
brocade
are four volumes of the
> Buddha's *Wisdom Discourses*---
>> Each volume consists of about 300
loose-leaf sheets of a pliant black material
> On which the Sanskrit text of the discourse
>> is meticulously inscribed in gold ink---According to
the priest and elders of
this temple
> these are the very volumes retrieved by Nagarjuna
>> from the subterranean lake

III.

Farther east in the Katmandu Valley
> resting among terraced fields of millet
>> Is a temple called Sankhu
a shrine to the tantric goddess Vajrayogini---
> All alone in meadow
>> behind the elegant cluster of buildings
is a chipped stone statute of a seated Buddha
> with a halo of 7 snakes---
>> The statue is identified as that of Nagarjuna--
The villagers treat with reverence
> of those for whom the gods are familiar
>> but cannot explain why it is there

Nagarjuna says:

If the gods were us
We would be eternal
For the gods are unborn in eternity---
Were we other than them
We would be ephemeral
Were we different
We would never connect

**Kamo River Mid-autumn**
Between buildings on the far bank
        Great red round moon rises
                Black lacquer river turns gold –
Later, moon is smaller, whiter
        River becomes silver beneath the
                dark form of Nijo Bridge across which
                      no traffic passes –
It shimmers like a school of white fish

**Things are not what they appear to be, nor are they otherwise**

   The fluted appearance of Okinawan cliffs
They look like accordions of stone
   the groove & spur architecture a result
     of 100s of parallel waterfalls
       that form with every rain –
The cliffs are *draped* with waterfalls after a storm
   From a distance the scale is deceiving
    Get close to the cliffs
&what looked like mere threads of
  falling water from a mile away
   turn out to be roaring
     cataracts 6 to 10 feet
        thick

## Gaijin

– Gaijin: usually translated as a foreigner, literally outside person; outside.

Hike into western foothills of Heian Kyo
Leave the path
A shortcut through the bamboo grove
And out the other side, someone's farm
Stop to rest, sit on a stone not far from
thatched roof house

On the porch a young girl
dressed in T-shirt and mompe, pantaloon-like pants perches on a
wooden crate of empty beer bottles
The tender points of her breasts
can be seen through the thin fabric of her T-shirt
A medallion gleams
in the hollow of her throat, A tiny disk frozen in silver –
She is perhaps twelve

It can only be her mother beside her,
a sun bronzed compact woman with braided black hair covered by a
straw coolie hat
The mama is peeling daikon, big white radishes
She saves the leafy heads in a shallow basket at her feet pauses to
wipe sweat from her brow with a pale pink cloth

The young girl has a can of green tea,
but she hasn't drunk much of it

She is worried about something:
It can be seen in the slump of her shoulders, in the sprawl of her thin legs
Several times her eyes shimmer with tears she is just able to control
When she looks up
It becomes clear that she is older than she-appeared at first, thirteen or fourteen
An air of naiveté, an awkwardness of limb and gesture makes her seem younger
She fidgets, and at last says, "Kachan (Mama)?" "Nani (what)?"
The mother's voice seems a beat too slow
It drags itself reluctantly past her lips
"Kaasan--is Ichiro just smoke and ashes?"
Mama is silent, searching for an answer that will satisfy and comfort
"Chottomite," she says looking in my direction. "Gaijin dakara."

Mother and daughter see me sitting on the stone in the break of the bamboo grove
I stand up, bow slightly; they bow back deeply

"Shitsureidesuga, nagai aida aruiteite, chotto yasumu'ndesukedo"
I answer in awkward Japanese, "I beg your pardon but I've been walking for a long time, took a rest here"
Their faces are now masks, blandly and shyly friendly for the sake of the gaijin
They will offer me hospitality, a can of cold tea maybe but I won't accept

Under the blazing blue bowel of the sky the daughter's eyes are downcast
wanting me to be gone
I nod, turn and walk back into the bamboo thicket
 A gaijin ghost

## Peace Plaza, Hiroshima

Japan, August 6 2005
The time: 10 minutes
past 8 in the morning—
    In exactly 5
minutes a bell will toll
to mark the moment
when the atomic bomb
exploded here—   8:10 and it's already
90 degrees—5 minutes
from now and 60 years
ago it was 10,000 degrees
in Peace Plaza, ground
zero, the hypocenter
--and here I sit in a
folding chair with 500
other people on this
spot 1,500 feet beneath
the detonation point,
looking at the empty rostrum—
Past the dais I can see
the iconic A-bomb racked
building left standing, and
the white cenotaph where
scores of unknown bodies
reduced to ashes lay—
To the right of the
dais sit the big shots, Koizumi the PM,
the government officials
from Europe, Russia, even
from the PRC and the ROK, victims
of Japan's aggression—
Where are the Americans?
Sitting with the rank & file,
all us peaceniks, Buddhists,
Methodists, Quakers—no official
acknowledgement from the US
government—maybe
for the best—

      The bell is tolling
8:15 AM—the sun's
exploding—

    *Notes: Koizumi: Junichiro Koizumi, prime minister of Japan 2001-2008. PRC: Peoples Republic of China. ROK: Republic of Korea.*

## A Man Who Lost His Hair and Died Bleeding

Atsumu Yamashita, age 20, was injured
        by the A-Bomb while doing demolition work—

He recovered from his injuries
        enough to walk around—

But soon he began bleeding from
        his nose—

He lost his hair—

He developed purple spots
        under his skin
and died vomiting blood at the end of August—

He was conscious and lucid
        to the end

        *– Hiroshima Peace Museum, August 4, 2005*

## The Forbidden Lunch Box

*(Displayed in Hiroshima Peace Museum but not allowed by the US Congress to be shown to the US public 1995 Smithsonian Institute.)*

Small rectangular metal
Lunch box, charred food
Visible
Said to be a mixture of rice
Barley and soy beans

The box looks remarkably clean
Scoured by atomic fire
A little battered but otherwise
Once fitted with a new lid
Usable

Belonged to Shigeru Orimen
First-year student at Second Hiroshima Prefectural Junior High School
He was exposed to the bomb at his building demolition work site
600 meters from the hypocenter

Every day with his classmates
He was mobilized to help with the demolition of buildings for fire lanes
On August 6, as usual, taking the lunch his mother had prepared
He left home early in the morning

After the A-bomb fell
His mother wandered through the ruins of Hiroshima looking for him
Early in the morning on August 9, on the bank of the HonkawaRiver
She found Shigeru's body with this lunch box held tight under his stomach
The lunch Shigeru never ate was charred black

By order of Congress
No victims allowed--

## Student Uniform

The body of second-year student Fukuoka Hajime
  aged 14 was never identified —
His mother went from place to place
  but no ashes could be confirmed as his —

The name-tag on his school uniform was discernable
  and the father of a classmate delivered it to the family —
    This was the only belonging of Hajime's that they
were able to confirm —

## Tricycle

Tetsutani Shinichi aged 3 years and 11 months
        was exposed to the A-bomb
While riding his tricycle in front of his house —
        He died the same day —
Shinichi's father couldn't bear to place a 3 year old
        alone in a distant grave —
            He buried Shinichi and his tricycle in the
backyard—

**Mother, Mother**

12 year old Ueda Masayuki escaped after the bombing
        to neighboring Fukushima-cho —
A neighbor happened to see him and help him —
            Burned so badly that skin hung from his whole body
                he could only cry, "Mother, mother!"—
        Masayuki died on the afternoon of the 8$^{th}$ without
seeing his mother —

## Geta (Wooden Sandal)

Miyoko Inoue, age 13, first year student at
Municipal Girls High School was 500 meters
from the hypocenter helping to clear a
fire lane—
Her mother searched for her day after day
but could never find
her corpse ---
3 months later this sandal
was found --
It was positively
identified as Miyoko's because the straps
were made from her mother's kimono –
After 60 years
the imprint of her left foot
remains visible –

*– Hiroshima Peace Museum August 6, 2005*

## 謎々 (Nazonazo)
## A Bar in Hiroshima

A girl bar with red
        neon, called "Riddle"
The young woman took a seat
        on the bar stool next to me
"Nihongo wadiajoubu?" she
asked me "Ee, diajoubuyo"

        A blast of cool air
chilled the sweat on my
        face
and carried her scent
        She smelled good
but I noticed the
        mamasan behind
            the bar
Why did she name the bar "Riddle"?

        The mamasan answers,
"It sounds exotic and it seems to
        pose a question about life"

She was eight when the bomb
        killed her mother and sister—
She still carries scars from
        the glass that slashed her body

## On the Lid of an Urn

I.

There are caskets in automobile hearses that glide gently
forward Followed by the long chain of the funeral procession
And there are coffins dragged along on screeching pushcarts
Tied down roughly with a common rope
There are people who gouge
Out the viscera of their dead
And then wait upon the mountains
For the birds
There are people who scale precipices, their
Dead stuffed into leather bags upon their backs
And there are secluded tombs away at the far ends
Well kept avenues of approach flanked with
Statues of lions and camels and of elephants
While by the shores of northern seas,are graves
Marked only by native rocks forever lashed by
Stormy waves

II.
Pictured on the cover of the Museum of
Natural History magazine
Is the lid of ajar
Except for the magazine's title, the whole cover is taken
Up by the face of a young Egyptian noblewoman, drawn big
Against a vermilion background
This is the lid of an urn used in ancient Egypt as a container for
The viscera of corpses to be mummified
The noble woman has a wig and her eyes are of obsidian and quartzite
A glass image of the
Sacred serpent had originally been attached to the forehead
Her loved ones left behind would have assembled before her
To mourn this dead woman

Some would have prayed, some would
Have waved incense censers, some would have made funeral
Offerings of great price
The lid of the alabaster urn would
Then have been removed and her internal organs
Gently placed within
What memories would have stirred then in those
People as lid met jar?

**– Young Research Library UCLA 1/01**

## Los Judíos Sefardíes Regresan

I.

It is hard to imagine, standing at the top of La Rambla, in the
multicolored swirl of overdressed tourists, Mexican hats and
Antonio Gaudí paraphernalia, that I'm walking with my aunt and
uncle, my cousins, recently returned from living in Mexican exileto
observe Yom Kippur this October 10, 1978
and that it was here in Barcelona on 19 July 1936 that
the opening shots were fired in what was to become the Spanish
Civil War

II.

October 5, 1938 Yom Kippur is celebrated in Barcelona
January 29, 1939 Barcelona falls to the fascists
May 1, 1940 the "Jewish Archive" is established
And the abbreviation "AJ" appears in the records of Jewish citizens
*"Se le supone la peligrosidadpropia de la razajudía (sefardita)"*
The word "Jew" would be written in red ink on permits issued to
Spanish Jews
And Spain's synagogues are shuttered

III.

Sephardic Jews, who, since their ancestors were expelled from Spain
in 1492
Spread through the centuries in a wide diaspora –
to the Ottoman Empire and the south of Italy;
to Spain's colonies in Central and South America;
and to outposts in what are now New Mexico, Texas and Mexico
while some continued to live an underground existence in their
Spanish motherland
The first Republican government of 1871 permitted the free practice
of religion
The Sepharadim opened their synagogues
And the 1934 Republican government allowed an immigration
reform
which opened the door to descendants of Sephardic Jews

After four decades of centralizing, Catholicizing Francoism
The new democratic government once again allowed freedom of religion
And the synagogues reopened

IV.

I walk with my relatives to this synagogue
One of 5 medieval synagogues still remaining
Against my will tears flow when I put on my keepah as I step through the entrance door--

V.

The core values of Yom Kippur--
repentance of my own sins against humanity and forgiveness of those who have sinned against me –
resonate really deeply for me in this synagogue
I have a lot of repentance and forgiveness to do, and I'll be mindful of that
Some rabbis describe Yom Kippur as the day you look out from the top of the mountain
you've been climbing all year, can see your life from that perspective,
and have the chance to make changes and become a better, more human person--
I'll aim for that
Love to you all.

## To Persevere

The wrecked black neighborhood I visited when I went to meetings with comrades at the library
was still suffering the aftermath of the uprising;
in retaliation the forces of white supremacy had arranged
for landlords, drug dealers, and arsonists to ravage it.
In the trailer park I walked through on my way home,
middle aged women wore skimpy clothes fashioned for emaciated models,
brazenly flaunting bodies the corporate media deemed more obscene than pornography;
I saw them as heroines in the struggle against patriarchal beauty norms.
The homeless were supposed to be the ultimate examples of failure;
they were heroes too –
No homeless person ever evicted anyone's grandmother from her home.

I saw them as comrades who refused to disgrace themselves for worthless prizes.
The shiftless hoboes and migrant workers who'd seen half the world on a dime,
The minimum wage employees who never wanted to be anyone's boss,
the workers at the cash registers with cameras pointed at them from all directions –
They are no less worthy than the big name social justice warriors
who write editorials for the *New York Times*.

If you want to subject yourself to a real test of mettle,
try failing.
Struggling to succeed can be demanding,
but failure is trying like nothing else.
Some of us have spent years, lifetimes, whole generations in failure and disappointment.
We know how much poverty, humiliation, suffering we can take –
we're well versed in these things, we've had plenty of practice.
We're not easily intimidated
We have nothing to lose

We persist with a patience that is inconceivable to celebrities, star athletes,
and spelling bee winners.
Just as the homeless woman who greets the dawn with her will to live in tact
after walking around all night to keep from freezing to death is
tougher than the most high-powered corporate financial shark,
we failures are better equipped than any other class to take
the risks one must take to change the world

## Anthropocene

*THANK YOU* Charles Lyell
you who distinguished between various layers of rock
determining the proportions of extinct and non-extinct fossils each
contained—

~CENE-Greek-KAINOS-RECENT

Miocene, MEIOS—FEW of the fossils are recent
Pliocene, PLEIOS—MORE of the fossils are recent
Pleistocene, PLEISTOS—MOST of the fossils are recent
Anthropocene, ANTHROPOS, man, human being--humankind is the
new geological force transforming the planet beyond recognition,
chiefly by burning prodigious amounts of coal, oil, and natural gas

ANTHROPOGENIC
Rapid melting of arctic sea ice
      reduction of the earth's albedo--

Melting of the frozen tundra in northern regions
      releasing methane (a much more potent greenhouse gas than
carbon dioxide) trapped
beneath the surface, causing accelerated warming--

Growing ocean acidification (from past carbon absorption)
      carbon build-up in the atmosphere and enhanced warming--

Extinction of species due to changing climate zones
      leading to the collapse of ecosystems dependent on these
species, and the death of still more species—

      TERMINAL CRISIS—a death of the whole anthropocene
          the period of human dominance of the planet

## More! More! More!

*Non-biodegradable substances are those which cannot be transformed into harmless natural state by the action of bacteria. And burning of these substances causes more pollution in the environment.*

Drink from that plastic water bottle
then throw it away!
It'll lay in the land fill 450 years
Who cares?
More plastic bags!
Toss 'em in the trash
so convenient, don't use 'em again
Nylons, chiffon dresses, stockings, ropes, umbrellas
use 'em 'til they wear out and throw them away
can't be re-cycled anyway!
Fresh unpolluted drinking water is rare?
Don't believe it, so leave those taps running all day
More herbicides, fungicides, pesticides
And chemical fertilizers too
use up all that phosphate rock!
Remove the forests
disappearing at a rate of 375 km each day
wash that top soil away!
Species are dying out 1,000 times faster than their natural rate of extinction?
Don't worry, we'll bring 'em back at Disneyland!

## MAGA MAGA

Climate change is fake science
The Proud Boys are the real heroes
The cops kill and me I say MAGA MAGA
The jester is king and me I sing MAGA MAGA
The bombs go off and me I scoff MAGA MAGA
Girls run and me I follow MAGA MAGA
The Russians tweet and me I dance MAGA MAGA
Ford denounces and the Senate shouts MAGA MAGA

It's the Big Check Book
that makes it all move—Make America Great Again!

**OBVIOUSLY, GENTLEMEN,**
IF YOU FEAR FOR THE MORALITY OF YOUR WIVES,
THE EDUCATION OF YOUR CHILDREN,
THE PEACE OF MIND OF YOUR INVESTORS,
THE SUBMISSIVENESS OF YOUR MISTRESSES AND HOUSEPETS,
THE SAFETY OF YOUR ARMCHAIRS AND PRIVATIZED PRISONS AND FACTORY FARMS,
THE MANNER IN WHICH YOUR WHOREHOUSES ARE LICENSED AND THE SECURITY OF THE STATE…
THEN YOU ARE RIGHT.

BUT WHAT CAN YOU DO?
YOU ARE ROTTEN,
AND THE FIRE HAS BEEN LIT.

## Twisted in Blood and Nerve

At the residential dwellings,
at the commercial edifices
everywhere in the city
where the riot drags on cold, dull and strong,
everywhere at the doors of our homes

Dull, to bring death;
blind, low, at the base of the earth,
blind, cold, of steel, of iron,
with the metal of their hate
elemental,

with their steel teeth ready to bite,
their clockwork,
wheels, nuts, springs,
their short black mouths on the mounts
squats

the thing of steel, of iron, inert, which mutilates in seconds,
 at the fatal moment of battle,
which digests seconds – tac-tac-tac –
the seconds drop to the infinite –
and lives tumble to the great cold of the tombs,

the machine which eats, tears, bursts, pierces, excavates
the flesh, becomes twisted in blood and nerves,
breaks the bones, makes the rails sing with the hollow of perforated
chests,
makes the brain ooze with the breaking of great faces
grey among blackened blood

Low machine to kill, everywhere, in the city of dull riot,
lurking at the doors of our homes,

watching for what wants to be born,
watching for what lifts from human hearts and from the depths of the live earth,
for what rises from burning faith, from mad hope and from anger –
from want and from light –
from enthusiasm and from prayer,
which goes up to flower – acts, cries – flames
low to cut down flight, the machine in ambush: victory to the people of iron laws,
victory to metal on flesh – and in the dream – the law of death.

## Trumpenvolk

They eat dead food with
false teeth --
Their buildings have
false fronts --
Their radio and television stations
broadcast dead air --
They kill time as spectators of
false images --
Their corporations trade in false advertising
Their employment "opportunities"
offer only murderous mistreatment
lethal boredom and fatal submission --
They demand that you meet deadlines
They ask you to give up your life for
their countries, their religions, their economies
-- They inhabit dead cities and
make false moves going nowhere at all treading
day after day
the same paths of despair --
Their system is organized
by artificial intelligence
and provides only virtual reality --
Their culture will pin you down
and bore you to death
their lifestyle is lifeless --
Their existence is a permanent deadlock
Everything about them is dead and false – Does
the dead end justify the means?
Even their air is conditioned

**The Perfect Ones**

The perfect ones
The beautiful ones
The right ones, the just ones, the noble ones
The ones who never break
down crying in restaurants,
who never do anything in secret that they would be ashamed of
The normal ones
The healthy ones
The ones who always plan ahead
The content ones
The happy ones
The ones who work hard
and reap the benefits,
who brush and floss after every meal
The well-adjusted ones
The popular ones
The ones who never disappoint,
who grow up to be president
The lucky ones
The ones with perfect skin and perfect teeth and perfect figures
The ones who want what they have and have what they want ---

They don't exist
The ones posing as them
 are even more fucked up than you.

## How Do You Want to Die?

Hanging from a rafter with the stool kicked to the floor beneath you?
From an overdose of sleeping pills,
like an actress or fed up house wife?
Opening your arteries with a razor,
in a hot bath so you won't shake so much when the warmth leaves your body?

All at once,
in a spatter of brains and bones at the concrete foot of the high rise
where you work?
Or in increments,
installment by installment with cigarettes and saturated fat and air pollution,
high blood pressure,
radiation,
 toxins in the water,
carcinogenic sugar substitutes and cell phones?

Do you want certainty,
a gun to your temple?
Or do you play the lottery – driving on the freeway stoned out of your mind,
having unprotected sex with strangers,
paying taxes to a government that might send the police to your door with guns in their hands?

Perhaps you're getting paid for it – how much are you worth per hour?
Do you wash dishes for minimum wage,
give and receive orders for a manager's salary,
fight your way to the top to get a fair price for your life?

Or are you buying it?

Do you purchase it in single servings,
buying yourself a taste whenever you can with alcohol, cocaine,
heroin,
prostitutes,
action movies,
video games,
television,
whatever it takes to go blank for an instant?

Do you sometimes long to cut right to the inevitable,
flinging yourself into the abyss of some addiction,
absolute negation of everything you ever wanted,
everything that has disappointed you?

Do you savor every drop, stretching it out as far as you can?
A moderate dose every day for the rest of your life,
with health insurance to make sure you don't miss out on a single hour?
Or are you ready to get it all over with,
consummate the affair with one defiant gesture,
flaunting your disdain for the tragedies of this world as you go down in a swarm of bullets?

Or maybe it's not death you're after, after all –

*But what else is there?*

**It comes to you in small**
fragments that hardly show
where it has entered
It comes, sometimes, atrociously –
It can come from spittle carried on the air, from unboiled
water, or it can come with a
terrific white-hot clanging
Roar
It comes in small crackling whispers that precede the
noise of an automatic weapon
It comes in the metallic
rending crash of a vehicle or
The simple lack of traction on
a slippery road
It comes in bed to most
people like love's opposite number –

We live with it all our lives
but we only pay attention
when it claims millions or when
It claims the ones we
love

## Endgame

When the rich have displaced ALL the poor from the urban core
banished them
from their neoliberal isotropic plane
from their plane of business immanence
have we not reached a strange apotheosis?
Have we not reached a sort of endgame
when the game is really up, even as we still feign the moves?
When, after the pawns have finally gone, have been sacrificed,
when little is left on the urban checkerboard besides kings,
kings playing off against other kings, square by square,
is there nothing left to win and no possibility of ever winning?
FIN DE PARTIE.

**You who no longer dance in the street**
Who have given up on winning
But not yet on giving in;
Have you made your peace with war?
Did they bribe you to betray
your scorn for bribery and betrayal?
Would you seek accommodation
with the ones who broke your heart
And trade the bitterness of struggle
For the poison of defeat?

**Capitulation is necessary only when struggle** has become completely
impossible and paralysis a form of annihilation.
When one is caught between resistance and self-abnegation,
playing a desperate game
destined to be duped, dishonored, rejected
when one becomes an obstacle to ambition,
duty requires seizing the final chance, even if it is the only one.
I reproach myself for justifying dubious, selfish
and vile adaptations and the
duplicity which hides them.
All of it exists like gangrene.
When one cannot escape from defeat,
submission is sometimes the last means of resistance.
Defeat leaves room only for duplicity,
reservations of conscience, secret defiance.
Some of my comrades, unacquainted with what
happened behind the scenes,
believe these distortions with a pure heart and
reply by spurning me,
while the opportunists, true to their nature,
distance themselves from the ranks of the fallen.
That agony is not my triumph but my defeat --

When your friends
misunderstand your works
and your enemies understand them

all too well –
When waking up
feels like a defeat
rather than a triumph –
When the razor blade or the .38 beckons,
remember –
Death is not pretty
only well advertised –

**Rimbaud knew better than**
to save any of himself for the grave--
He spent every resource to the last penny--
He burned
money, health, friends, family, sanity
as so much fuel for the fire—

When Death came to take the poet
He got nothing, not even a man
with his pride or common sense in tact--
When He comes for me
What will He find?

## Wage Slave

Almost every member of my
extended family --
grandparents, parents,
aunts, uncles, cousins --
were wage laborers
in the Old Country and the New
World they mined coal,
hauled steel, labored on construction
sites and as office secretaries,
served the wealthy as domestic
workers, clerked in company
stores, cleaned offices and homes,
took in laundry, even danced topless
in Vegas floorshows --
I joined the work force at 15 and have
been at it ever since, working
as a dish washer, fry cook, telemarketer,
movie extra, baby sitter,
movie projectionist, serigrapher, artist's model,
landscape hand, proof reader, ESL teacher,
program manager, magazine editor, executive
director of a venerable arts non-profit --
And now, in old age I'm
washing dishes again --

## FOR/AGAINST

For workers on the line bored, tired and robbed of their creative days;

For women raped, pinched, door-opened, decultured, feminized, beaten, married;

For Blacks, Latinos, Native Americans, Asians, Queers...nameless, robbed of dignity, lynched, harassed, low-paid, running, jailed;

For the drunks and addicts, the worn-out and the never lively, for the old and ill who should be long-lived and wise;

For the young, schooled and unschooled, enduring boredom,

Getting stoned, stealing sex and losing love, trying to escape or trying to find a way in:

For those on welfare or off, looking in or looking out, employed or unemployed alone or in pairs, hiding their sex or flaunting it, angry, sad, mad;

For all those who feel less than they could feel, for those who are less than they could be in this rich land, the United States of America; and,

For the Puerto Rican, Chilean, Argentinian, South African, Libyan, Iranian, Syrian, Pakistani and Ukrainian exploited, robbed, starved, cheated, tortured, ambushed, kidnapped, death squadded;

For all the world's citizens suffering brutality and indignity--the electric shocks and murdered relatives, the starvation and the working for pennies, the military boot and the cultural stamp--

For the empire's citizens; and,

For the empire's enemies:

For the strikers, the saboteurs, the feminists and

anarchists, the Marxists and nationalists, for those with no ideology but liberty;

For the memory of Durruti and the Spanish freedom fighters;

For the memory of Cabral and the liberation of Africa;

For the memory of Victor Serge and the Russians in revolt, for Luxembourg and the German left,

For Black Lives Matter, Antifa, Women's Liberationists, Farm Workers, Puerto Rican Nationalists, for those of AIM and their

Relatives who resisted and died in the past and who nonetheless live on

For the ones who dodged the draft, for those who went and

Disrupted, and for those who went and died—or lived;

For the French in the streets of May and the Italians in Autumn, for the Mexicans in the summer and Kurds and Chinese…

For everyone who has fought, fights, or will fight for a better

World than they were, are, or are going to be bequeathed;


And at the same time, necessarily:
Against the Trumps, Kochs and Putins, the elite CIA of the world, and the Kissingers all;

Against the doctors who deal in dollars but not in dignity, the landlords, the lawyers, and the politicians with eyes closed to injustice;

Against the owners, administrators, bosses, rapists and racists, those on top and those who aspire only to be there;

Against the dealers of bad hands;

Against the social ties and unties that breed the good and

the bad, that breed the pain and we who grow ugly by inevitably "benefitting" from its continuance;

And last, for after all this is to be a poem;

Against the poets who keep art as if it were their private property, who enshrine their own ignorance under false halos, who can justify barbarism or technically dissect it as their interests require--but who never shed a tear;

Against the media liars, the news pimps, the career thinkers, the academics who propagate propaganda to preserve this system the academics who call for justice and always do nothing, the ones who succeed but don't stay angry, the ones that don't really care; it is time for all of us on the outs to talk of what a better world could--will--really be like, that we might together make it so.

Till when there will be fewer acquaintances and many more friends, lovers and first and last;

To those who have yet to live under economic equality

I dedicate this poem.

## Go Underground

After the defeat of the Paris Commune,
Arthur Rimbaud, a 17-year-old poet-protagonist,
said the blood of its victims drained away all hope for his generation.
For a long time to come, Rimbaud said,
truth will have to go underground.
It had been reduced to tatters, along with life.
Once again truth has similarly been reduced to tatters,
along with life.

To trace out any hope of its recovery
poets need to organize underground
follow Old Mole of old
agitate underground
assemble in low rent store fronts
in sunken basements
maybe in communal squats
somewhere cheap
somewhere far away.
Or perhaps close by.

Begin again. Build up again.
Truth today is more truthful in the underground than in
the commercial overground or in
the non-profit overground.
Truth will not be voiced from the rich core, but
from the honest poor periphery
from the margins of life
from the margins of our cities
from its grungy peripheral outskirts
from broken-down informal zones à défendre, defended to the end.
There, nothing will be truer than nothingness
the source of a new radical beginning.

**You can taste it in the shock and roar**
of a first, unexpected kiss,
or in the blood in your mouth
that instant after an accident when you realize you're still alive.
It blows in the wind you feel on the rooftops of a really reckless
night of adventure.
You hear it in the magic of your favorite songs,
how they lift and transport you in ways
that no science or psychology could ever account for.
It might be you've seen evidence of it scratched into bathroom
walls in a code without a key,
or you've been able to make out a pale reflection of it
in the movies they make to keep us entertained.
It's in between the words when we speak of our desires and
aspirations,
still lurking somewhere beneath the limitations of being
"practical" and "realistic."
When poets and revolutionaries stay up until sunrise,
wracking their brains for the perfect sequence of words or deeds
to fill hearts (or cities) with fire,
they're trying to find a hidden entrance to it.
When children escape out the window to go wandering late at
night,
or freedom fighters search for a weakness in government
fortifications,
they're trying to sneak into it.
They know better than us where the doors are hidden.
When teenagers vandalize a billboard to provoke all-night
chases with the police,
or anarchists interrupt an orderly demonstration to smash the
windows of a corporate chain store,
they're trying to storm its gates.
When you're making love and you discover a new sensation or

region of your lover's body,
and the two of you feel like explorers discovering a new part of
the world on a par with a desert oasis or the coast
of an unknown continent,
as if you are the first ones to reach the north pole or the moon,
you are charting its frontiers.
It's not a safer place than this one —
on the contrary, it is the sensation of danger there that brings us
back to life:
the feeling that for once, for one moment that seems to eclipse
the past and future,
there is something real at stake.
Maybe you stumbled into it by accident, once, amazed at what
you found.
The old world splintered behind and inside you,
and no physician or metaphysician could put it back together
again.
Everything before became trivial, irrelevant, ridiculous as the
horizons
suddenly telescoped out around you and undreamed-of new
paths offered themselves.
And perhaps you swore that you would never return,
that you would live out the rest of your life electrified by that
urgency, in the thrill of discovery and transformation —
but return you did.
Common sense dictates that this world can only be experienced
temporarily,
that it is just the shock of transition, and no more;
but the myths we share around our fires tell a different story:
we hear of women and men who stayed there for weeks, years,
who never returned, who lived and died there as heroes.
We know, because we feel it in that atavistic chamber of our

hearts that holds the memory of freedom
from a time before time, that this secret world is near,
waiting for us.
You can see it in the flash in our eyes,
in the abandon of our dances and love affairs,
in the protest or party that gets out of hand.
You're not the only one trying to find it.
We're out there, too…
some of us are even waiting there for you.
And you should know that anything you've ever done or
considered doing to get there is
not crazy, but beautiful, noble, necessary.
Revolution is simply the idea we could enter that secret world
and never return;
or, better, that we could burn away this one, to reveal the one
beneath entirely.

## After the Cataclysm
*– for S.A. Griffin*

Truth will get communicated via old means not new media.
It will be shared by word of mouth and on paper, not online.
Current social media is saturated, there is
too much of it --
too much of it peddling lies, and fear and loathing,
too much commercial media play
too many channels that offer people
too little choice.
A new underground truth will emerge like it once did,
from smart people living off very little,
living in ruined and cheap neighborhoods,
communicating via old experimental media.
And there will be cafés and hang outs
where kindred spirits and fellow travelers can
commune with one another,
bump into one another,
talk and argue with one another,
share sounds together,
maybe play some old jazz riffs.
They can be present, in person,
and engage in old debates about the future,
and have direct human encounters not mediated screen encounters.
New reparatory theaters will emerge, reenacting old plays by
Beckett or Brecht or by new Living Theatre troupes,
putting fresh spins on old staples, reinventing a
new vanguard, inspiring

new audiences while reenergizing old ones
who have not entirely forgotten what it was like the first time around.
What would begin again is a new Poetry Underground,
where a new critical culture can be incubated,
a will to live differently, like it did before,
making our cities interesting and democratic again. Or
perhaps it will not happen.
Perhaps nothing like this will ever happen. Not again.
Perhaps it is no longer possible for poetry to go on, having lost so much.
Try again with the old answers? Fail again, fail better?
And even if poetry cannot go on, it will go on—maybe for another five thousand years.

## Scott Wannberg: Poet and Cinephile

Scott Wannberg is widely known as poet but he was also a cinephile. Cinephilia infused many of his poems, and his movie references carried more weight and meaning than mere pop cultural color. When I first met Scott in 1995 after reading his work for 25 years in various small press zines, I noticed that he peppered his rapid-fire conversations with allusions to character actors, obscure movies and even more obscure directors. It was the sort of repartee that only a cinephile would understand, and when we were introduced by my friend poet Amelie Frank at a reading at Sam's Book City in North Hollywood, California I answered Scott's cinematic references in kind. He paid attention and soon the two of us were talking intimately about our favorite films. I felt that I had a good sense of the man through his poetry but I didn't appreciate the depth of his genius mind until this one-on-one conversation.

Over the years since that first face to face meeting, we saw each other often at poetry readings, movie screenings, parties and for awhile every weekday morning on the #14 Santa Monica bus on our way to work at our respective jobs. Now Scott was a big man, a tall man and in a crowded room he often spotted me before I saw him and would invariably boom out my name "RICHARD MODIANO!" to which I would answer "SCOTT WANNBERG!" We played this game on the bus too and drew looks from annoyed, puzzled or bemused fellow passengers.One Friday morning on the bus we had our usual conversation that covered movies, poetry, politics and literary gossip. Scott said, "Hey, are you going to the Cinematheque tonight to see Boetticher?" "I'm going if I can get a ride. Are you?" "I'm going if I can get a ride."

"Boetticher" is Budd Boetticher, one of Scott's favorite directors. We both loved Boetticher's Westerns. In the late 1950s Boetticher directed six B westerns which became known as the Renowned cycle. The combination of the moral certitude and compulsion of their heroes, the sparse terrain in which the films were shot, and Boetticher's simple, unobtrusive shooting style heralded a new and influential era of the Western. That series, mostly produced by Harry Joe Brown, written by Burt Kennedy and starring Randolph Scott, comprised *7 MenFrom Now* (1956), *The Tall T* (1957), *Decision At Sundown* (1957), *Buchanan Rides Alone* (1958), *Ride Lonesome* (1959), and *Comanche Station* (1960.) *7 Men From Now* was one of Scott's favorite Boetticher movies. He even wrote a fine poem about Boetticher that was issued as a broadside by S. A. Griffin and given away free at the dedication of Beyond Baroque's bookstore, now known as The Scott Wannberg Bookstore and Poetry Lounge. (That poem comes at the end of this memoir.)

Well, we got our rides and met up at theAmerican Cinematheque on Hollywood Boulevard to see *Comanche Station* and then hear Budd Boetticher answer questions after the screening. A big man like Scott, Boetticher was 84 years old at the time old but looked 20 years younger. The Q & A was over, a few people were leaving the auditorium while fans surrounded the great director. Scott wanted to meet him so he plowed forward and parted the crowd like a ship cutting though Arctic ice and I followed in his wake. He stood in front of Boetticher and shook his hand and then rattled off Budd's complete filmography replete with pithy comments on each title. Boetticher was amazed and pleased, and at the end of Scott's discourse turned to his companion, cinematographer William Fraker, and said, "I think I've just met my greatest fan." Whereupon Scott pushed me forward and said, "This is Richard Modiano, your second greatest fan!"

## El Matador
### – for Budd Boetticher

yeah baby
Randy Scott's rainy vengeful back to the camera lens
in the opening number of
Seven Men From Now
Carlos Arruza
Mexico
one good shot of something singularly strong, amigo spare
low key director of genre jazz
Henry Silva telling Randy the kid is dead in the well in The
Tall T your excellent version of an Elmore Leonard story
having your child, Bullfighter and the Lady,
raped by BATJAC and John Wayne and John Ford
Mexico
one good shot of all those songs
you and Burt Kennedy helped redefine the
American Western in the fifties
and Randolph Scott got gnarly
you dance barefoot now
across the storyteller's hoedown
El Matador indeed
yeah baby
for Budd Boetticher
a visionary and a rhythm


– Scott Wannberg
12/07/01

## Poem for Rob Plath

Walk outside if you can –
or go to a window and open it.
Close your eyes
and sniff the air.
Listen –
What do you hear
calling on the wind?
Are the birds singing?
Are the crows cawing?
Do you hear
the rhythmic throb
of city traffic?
The cycling trill
of car alarms?
the cry of children
At play?
Open your eyes –
see the patterns
of light and shadows
the play of the wind.
begin your education
in the language
of nature.

**A Word**
    *– for Iris Berry*

You have to select a word
*It will be talked about as little as possible*
and have a deep suggestiveness like nature,
bloom from within itself,
and at the edge of the fate encircling you
it will become darkly and sweetly ripened

Of a hundred experiences it always
will be the sum total of only one --
One tear drop
becomes the harvest all tear drops,
a single point of red neon on Hollywood Blvd.
on a dark evening
is the light of the whole world

And after that your poem
like a substance entirely fresh,
released far away from your memory,
the same as a chord plucked from a Stratocaster,
the same as haze over the San Fernando Valley in spring,
will suddenly begin to sing from its own recollection

## More About the Book

After assuming the post of executive director of Beyond Baroque Literary/Arts Center Richard Modiano rapidly rose to the challenge of not only maintaining Beyond Baroque's relevance as a poetry laboratory for the greater Los Angeles area, but also of fostering a vibrant resurgence that re-established Beyond Baroque as an absolutely necessary literary resource for the entire West Coast. The value of his tireless efforts to encourage new work and ideas — before, during, and after his tenure — and to ensure that Beyond Baroque reflects the diversity and cultural life of the Venice community, cannot be overestimated. We continue to be truly fortunate to have his inspiration as a leader and as a poet.
~Viggo Mortesnsen, poet, actor, publisher

Charles Bukowski once wrote "a poem is a city / a poem is a city filled with streets and sewers / filled with saints, heroes, beggars, madmen…" and in these poems—and prose—we meet Richard Modiano's city and its inhabitants. Poets and film directors, bar denizens, baristas, and more—Modiano delves into the essence of their psyche in his writing about shared moments. Modiano writes with passion, emotion, and clarity, and these poems paint a formidable picture of the working class of the City of Angels that is as driven as a downtown bus and as engaging as the kind of film that makes you sigh, cry, and smile. Highly recommended.
~Kat Georges, poet, *Our Lady of the Hunger*

Richard Modiano creates irresistible flows and rhythms that steal your breath, exquisitely portraying places and people who live in a world we both long for and wish to forget. And yet, what makes Modiano's voice so necessary and wise is not mere brilliance, but gentleness, respect—its determination to leave no mark upon its surroundings except the promise of more just and human existence.
~Ryka Aoki, author *Seasonal Velocities* and *He Mele a Hilo*.

A taut, no nonsense but lyrical, expression of the poet's personal values, his underlying political purity and drive, the worker, the revolutionary; modesty pervades these deceptively simple observations, these revelatory expressions of self as if described by others with a critical eye, outwardly apparent scenes condensed into precise words of the most intimate

personal details, the poet's world spread before us in a few careful lines of heartrending beauty and unsparing honesty, to share and surprise us with our own recognition of reality, which comes as news; as James Joyce might have said, and did say about his own work, "It is time the ... people had a look at themselves in my highly polished looking glass." I was surprised to find myself in these poems by Richard Modiano.
~Ronee Blakely, singer-songwriter, composer, actress

Historically, Richard Modiano's knowledge of the LA poetry scene is nonpareil and his love of individuals is a constant that enhances our own ability to love. If you know nothing of Richard Modiano then read his unflinching work. There, on the page, you'll find a dear friend.
~Peter Carlaftes Publisher, Editor, Author, Poet, Playwright

I have always been a fan of the poetry of Venice's Richard Modiano. His poems are made from the sweat and grit of the real world. His imagery is fresh, his subject matter unique, and his attention is always laser focused upon the details of what is right and just. I find much to enjoy and contemplate in these exquisite poems of everydayness, community politics and urban life in the City of Angels. Richard's work is alive. I very highly recommend *The Forbidden Lunch Box*.
~M. L. Liebler, Detroit Poet & Director of The Detroit Writers' Guild.

As Richard Modiano writes, "I walk to the edge of night." In this engrossing collection of poems written over several decades, he observes the joys and failures of both personal and world history. A reminder of the necessity of art, learning, and curiosity.
~Jane Ormerod, poet and publisher

From feral cats in sick avocado trees , to a dream of Bela Lugosi, to the intimacy of his brother's deathbed , to a bar called Riddle in Hiroshima City, to Rimbaud's burning candle-like exit, Richard Modiano at once has the scope of Kerouac, the attention to detail and simplicity of Williams and the compression of Basho. This is a book of poems that exudes Camus' moving sentiment of "live to the point of tears." I haven't been excited for a collection like this in years.
~Rob Plath, author of *Feed These Words To The Buddha Who Is Slowly Waking Up Inside Of You*

Richard Modiano's poems are about poetry making a difference. They don't tell us this; they show us. The scenes they conjure place you right there, inside the action, whether it is waiting for a loved one to die, watching people you will never see again swaying with the motion of a subway train, on a one-night stand during a Greyhound bus layover in Cheyenne, Wyoming. In "After the Cataclysm," Modiano writes: ". . . Even if poetry cannot go on, it will go on—maybe for another five thousand years." These poems are good enough to keep that promise!
~Margaret Randall, author of *I Never Left Home: Poet, Feminist, Revolutionary* and *Out of Violence into Poetry.*

Richard Modiano's poems resonant with the simplicity and subtlety of the Japanese forms he knows so well. Each poem presents a specific moment and place, creating a personal center of identity that echoes with cultural memory. Each scene seems to appear and dissolve like the river of history. This is a brilliant and deeply affecting collection of poetry.
~Susan Suntree, writer, poet, teacher, author *Sacred Places*

In Richard Modiano's poem, "On the Streets of the Lower East Side," he writes, what could be his poetics:

> "Fearless knowledge
> of our capacity to hurt
> of our potential to love
> of our creative generosity."

Richard has been generous, gracious in his poetry, work, spirit. His poetry is lyrical, clear-eyed, contains violent breakage at times; it's poignant, loving, elegiac and compassionate.

A superlative poet, Richard Modiano.

~ Harry E. Northup

**Richard Modiano** is a native of Los Angeles. He attended the University of Hawai'i and New York University. While a resident of New York City he became active in the literary community connected to the Poetry Project where he came to know Gregory Corso, Allen Ginsberg, Anne Waldman, William S. Burroughs and Ted Berrigan. In 2001 he was a programmer at Beyond Baroque Literary/Arts Center, joined the Board of Trustees in 2006 and from 2010 to 2019, he served as Executive Director. In that time he produced and curated hundreds of literary events. Richard is a rank and file member of the Industrial Workers of the World. In 2019 he was elected Vice President of the California State Poetry Society and he was the recipient of the Joe Hill Award for labor poetry in 2022.

## More Books on Punk Hostage Press

Danny Baker
    *Fractured* – 2012
A Razor
    *Better Than a Gun in A Knife* Fight - 2012
    *Drawn Blood: Collected Works*
    *From D.B.P.LTD., 1985-1995* - 2012
    *Beaten Up Beaten Down* - 2012
    *Small Catastrophes in A Big World* - 2012
    *Half- Century Status* - 2013
    *Days of Xmas Poems* - 2014
    *Puro Purismo* - 2021
Iris Berry
    *The Daughters of Bastards* - 2012
    *All That Shines Under the Hollywood Sign* – 2019
    *The Trouble with Palm Trees* - 2021
    *Gas Station Etiquette* - 2022
C.V. Auchterlonie
    *Impress* - 2012
Yvonne De la Vega
    *Tomorrow, Yvonne - Poetry & Prose for Suicidal Egoists* - 2012
Carolyn Srygley- Moore
    *Miracles Of the Blog: A Series* - 2012
Rich Ferguson
    8th & Agony -2012
Jack Grisham
    *Untamed* -2013
    *Code Blue: A Love Story* ~ Limited Edition—2014
    *Pulse of the World. Arthur Chance, Punk Rock Detective* - 2022
Dennis Cruz
    *Moth Wing Tea* - 2013
    *The Beast Is We* - 2018
Frank Reardon
    *Blood Music* - 2013
Pleasant Gehman
    *Showgirl Confidential*—2013
    *Rock 'N' Roll Witch: A Memoir of Sex Magick, Drugs, And Rock 'N' Roll* - 2022
Hollie Hardy
    *How To Take a Bullet and Other Survival Poems*—2014
SB Stokes
    *History Of Broken Love Things*—2014

## More Books on Punk Hostage Press

Joel Landmine
    *Yeah, Well...*—2014
    *Things Change* - 2022
Michele McDannold
    *Stealing The Midnight from A Handful of Days*—2014
A.D. Winans
    *Dead Lions*—2014
S.A. Griffin
    *Dreams Gone Mad with Hope* - 2014
Nadia Bruce-Rawlings
    *Scars* - 2014
    *Driving in The Rain* - 2020
Lee Quarnstrom
    *WHEN I WAS A DYNAMITER, Or, how a Nice Catholic Boy Became a Merry Prankster, a Pornographer, and a Bridegroom Seven Times* - 2014
Alexandra Naughton
    *I Will Always Be Your Whore/Love Songs for Billy Corgan* - 2014
    *You Could Never Objectify Me More Than I've Already Objectified Myself* -2015
Maisha Z Johnson
    *No Parachutes to Carry Me Home* - 2015
Michael Marcus
    *#1 Son and Other Stories* - 2017
Danny Garcia
    *LOOKING FOR JOHNNY, The Legend of Johnny Thunders* - 2018
William S. Hayes
    *Burden of Concrete* - 2020
Todd Moore
    *Dillinger's Thompson* - 2020
Dan Denton
    *$100-A-Week Motel* – 2021

Jack Henry
    *Driving W/ Crazy, living with madness*—2021
Joe Donnelly
    *So Cal: Dispatches from the End of The World*—2022
Patrick O'Neil
    *Anarchy at The Circle K – On the Road with Dead Kennedys, TSOL, Flipper, Subhumans and... Heroin* – 2022

www.ingramcontent.com/pod-product-compliance
Lightning Source LLC
Chambersburg PA
CBHW031421160426
43196CB00008B/1010